HOLY HABITATION

Andrea Tellison
Holy Habitation

Published by Spines
ISBN: 979-8-89383-969-2

Spines

HOLY HABITATION

ANDREA TELLISON

CHAPTER I

FROM PAIN TO PURPOSE

I was born into a Christian family in 1967. My mother relocated to Houston, TX, after completing her requites at Southern University to attend nursing school. My father came to Texas Southern University and was then drafted into the Army for the Vietnam War. My mother told me she met my father on the bus headed to school, and he harassed her every day until she agreed to go on a date with him.

Upon returning from the war, he went back to Houston to pursue his passion for golf and his love for my mom. I was told by my parents and grandmother that my father was a tall, slim man before going to war. My grandmother told me that he came to her house with flowers to visit my mom, and she did not recognize him; he had become so muscular that he was no longer the skinny red-haired boy with green eyes but a very handsome man.

Of course, my parents resumed dating and eventually married, and I was born as the first grandchild on both sides of my family. When I was 44 years old, my father revealed to me that when I was a baby, they took me to his family Church to be Christened (dedicated to God). An older lady, an elder of the Church who had been a member there her whole life, approached and decreed that I would be a prophet for God for this nation. Because of this prophetic word, my family united to train me up in the Lord, and most of my childhood activities took place in and around Church. When I was five years old, my mother became pregnant with my sibling, and I, as well as my entire family, was elated..I was six when my baby brother was born.

After giving birth, my mother suffered from postpartum depression, which went misdiagnosed for many years. This began a process and cycle of pain within my family that disrupted the love and unity we had once known. My mother was eventually diagnosed with paranoid schizophrenia. I watched her go in and out of psychiatric hospitals until her passing away. This ravaged my family for over 30 years and had a devastating effect on us all. The trauma that my brother and I experienced as young children would shape our lives for many years. Unbeknownst to me, all of these painful events would become the pathway to prepare me for the ministry in which I am operating today: deliverance from demonic oppression or possession. As one could imagine, these events propelled me to develop an intimate relationship with the Lord Jesus Christ, trusting and believing that He would heal my mother and make her whole.

By the time I was a teenager, disappointment in not seeing this dream realized led me into rebellion and down some very dangerous paths. I became a teen mother, became addicted to drugs, and landed in a very dysfunctional and abusive relationship. By the time I was 26 years old, I had six children with this man and sought a way of escape. My father and grandparents placed me in a treatment facility, where I was able to overcome drug addiction after a suicide attempt. I can clearly remember saying to the Lord, almost in a dare, "If you are who I've been taught you are, and you are truly real, please help me or let me come to be with you because I'm tired—tired of being hurt, disappointed, and heartbroken." I am so grateful today that the Lord answered my prayer and demonstrated to me that He is truly real and that He still meets people in the pigpen. This book is dedicated to my love for the Lord and the many things He has delivered me from. My heart is that it will encourage and enlighten others to the realities of a relationship with the Lord and the hosting of His Holy Spirit.

While in the treatment facility, one of the staff members invited me and other ladies to go to Church with her. She was a member of Lakewood Church, under the leadership of the late John Osteen at that time. This was in 1993. To my surprise, the Lord was truly answering my prayer and beginning to lead me on the journey back to Him and into my true destiny and purpose. I am forever thankful for His love for me and the many people He has used along the way to bring forth His will in my life.

I felt a tug on my heart to receive prayer from Pastor John Osteen of Lakewood Church during an altar call to rededicate my life to the Lord. As he prayed for me, he placed his hand on my head, and about an hour later, I awakened, confused about what had transpired. Several friends informed me that I had been "knocked out." As they lifted me to my feet to leave the now-ended service, I was unaware that I had received an impartation or a measure of the Holy Spirit.

CHAPTER 2

A TRANSFORMATIVE ENCOUNTER

In 2005, I was praying for one of my children, crying out to the Lord to show me how to help her. She was in pain, which led to her rebellious acting out. While on my knees praying for her, an unusual thing happened: all of a sudden, an unknown power overtook me, rising up within me. Suddenly, I began to speak in an unknown language, and the power coursing from my mouth and body was beyond my understanding. I jumped up and ran into the bathroom to look at myself in the mirror. Because of the years spent experiencing my mother's battle with mental illness, coupled with many traumatic events in my life, I wondered if I was having a nervous breakdown. I was baffled but able to think; however, I had no control over my mouth. I tried to stop speaking, but I was powerless. I thought maybe if I went outside, it would stop. But it didn't. As I stood there, bewildered, I noticed my neighbor working in his garden, observing me as I almost shouted in an unknown language. In my mind, I wanted to ask him for help, but I couldn't speak in English. So, I ran back into the house and again looked in the mirror, feeling utterly undone. I began pacing around the house, realizing I was so afraid that I actually wanted to run from myself or whatever this force was that had consumed me.

This went on for several hours. By this time, I had submitted to this force and allowed it to have its way. Initially, I was so panicked that I couldn't even think straight, but as I yielded to the force, I realized I was not going crazy. The thought popped into my mind to call my oldest daughter for what I now recognize as help (smile). How silly I was; I was so uninformed when what I had been praying for had arrived. I called my daughter at work, where she was a bank teller at the time. Although she was not supposed to be on the phone, I knew she would recognize my voice. She answered and said, "Mama, hold on a minute," then proceeded to go to the restroom. When she got there, she asked, "Mama, are you okay?" She knew it had to be important since our family had agreed to text because she couldn't answer her phone at work. I proceeded to speak in this unknown language. My daughter immediately exclaimed, "Terrorists got my mama?" She said, "I'm on my way."

I hung up and proceeded to walk around the house, speaking this unknown language. Shortly after, my daughter arrived. As she walked into the house, she asked, "What is that in this house?" while I was still speaking in tongues. I was terrified because I had no control over my mouth and was trying to communicate with her using hand gestures at this point, as I could not speak in English—only in an unknown tongue. My daughter asked, "Have you been baptized by the Holy Spirit like the people in the Bible? I could feel the presence of the Lord when I walked in." [Acts 2:1-4] That's when it dawned on me what was actually happening, and I became elated. She asked, "How long have you been like this? Can you write?" I nodded my head yes and began to communicate with her by writing down what I'd experienced and that this had been going on for almost four hours. She asked, "What is it that you need me to do?" I asked her to go and pick up her siblings from school because what would I look like picking up my kids when I'm unable to speak properly? She left and came back with the kids. The kids entered and were immediately scared when they saw me, as they could also feel the presence of the Lord. They ran upstairs. My daughter explained to them what was going on because she hadn't said anything beforehand, and the kids didn't understand. After several more hours, my scared son came downstairs with a poster board saying, "Can you cook and talk to God at the same time? Because we're hungry." The joy of the Lord is our strength. This went on for about twelve hours until I went to bed. The power of the Holy Spirit was so strong that it literally exhausted me.

The next morning, when I woke up, I was afraid to do my daily devotion because this was how all of this had started. So, I proceeded to take the kids to school, came back home, and called my pastor to tell him what had happened because I needed insight. He explained that it was a blessing, a spiritual gift, and a promise from our Father in Heaven. He said that it's a prayer language. He explained to me, "Though you may not understand it, God understands exactly what you're saying. It's called praying in the Spirit." Then he told me to read some scriptures and that the Holy Spirit would teach me how to use the gift. [1 Corinthians 12] And as he said, the Holy Spirit began to teach me how to steward the gift!

From that point on, I began to incorporate the use of this gift into my daily prayer life. After that event, I started to notice that during speaking engagements and times of worship, I was becoming familiar with the person of the Holy Spirit. This encounter with the Holy Spirit also activated gifts in several of my children. They began to have prophetic dreams and visions. One of these dreams was given to my oldest daughter, who told me I had been baptized in the Spirit. In the dream, the Lord appeared to her as her grandmother, my mother, who had already transitioned to Heaven. She informed her to tell me that something was wrong with my car. The next morning, my daughter called me and said, "I had a dream, and grandma told me to tell you that something is wrong with your car." She was very serious and said grandma was insistent that I shouldn't drive my car. After speaking with my daughter, I called my spiritual mom to tell her what my daughter had just told me. She was there with me when I found my mother deceased. I was very doubtful, thinking there was nothing wrong with my car. Her advice to me was to take the car to get analyzed so that my daughter wouldn't worry. At that time, I owned a business and worked a second job in the evening that required me to travel quite a distance. I supervised a facility for people suffering from addiction and HIV/AIDS. I proceeded to take my car to the shop, and upon arrival, the mechanic asked what was wrong with my car. Because of my doubtfulness and the fact that I didn't want him to think I was crazy, I told him I just wanted it checked because I traveled late at night home from work. He told me to have a seat in the waiting area while he ran a diagnostic on my car. About forty-five minutes later, he came to give me the analysis. He said, and I quote, "God Himself must've sent you here." Little did he and I know, God actually had. In the diagnostic, he said that the front axle of my car was cracked, which was a serious problem. He proceeded to tell me the cost, and I told him I didn't have the money and that I would bring the car back on Friday. He said, "No ma'am, I can't do that. It's against the law for me to allow you to leave in the car now due to the danger associated with this problem. I'll keep the keys." I told him that I had to leave for work, but he insisted that I leave without the car. He informed me that one of the employees could take me home and told me it was best to get my belongings out of the car. When I got home, I called both my spiritual mom and my daughter and told them that the dream was, in fact, true and that my car had been impounded by the manager at Firestone Auto Repair. The guys would not allow me to leave in the car. After being dropped off at home and having time to sit quietly, I realized that God was mindful of me. [Psalm 8:4]After this prophetic protection was revealed, I continued on with my very full life. My spiritual mom had always said, "You have always had more to carry than most of us." I always said this, not realizing that I was actually speaking prophetically over my own life. "To whom much is given, much is required." Oh, how I would later learn the ramifications of those statements. I began to become more aware of and comfortable with the Holy Spirit in my private prayer and worship time, asking the Lord to lead me in building the business He had blessed me with, a business I had no formal training in. I stepped out in faith, and He led me step by step in learning this business, opening and operating it for over three years at that time. I promised Him I would "Never Forget" the theme song of my life, which was also one of my favorite worship songs by the great gospel singer Yolanda Adams. For all He had delivered me from and walked me through, I promised

Him I would be a blessing to everyone I could. Twelve years prior to this time in my life, I had been talking with the Lord, asking Him to teach me to be the best mother I could be, to father my children and, if He would, I knew I could make it through the season of raising 6 children as a single parent. Now, many years later, I was praying for one of these children when Holy Spirit came.

Several months after the dream was revealed to my oldest daughter, protecting our lives concerning the car, my youngest daughter received a vision from the Lord instructing her to tell me, "Success has been bestowed upon you." I received this Word with less doubt due to the previous occurrences; however, I still did not yet fully understand Father God, though I had attended Church most of my life. I believed this Word to be the answer to my private prayer, asking Him to help me build the company—a request my daughter was, of course, unaware of, as I had prayed this in the secret place with Him. Now my children were growing up and becoming more expensive to care for, so I placed my attention on expanding the business. Believing I had confirmation from Heaven that it would succeed, I didn't yet understand that this success, from the Lord's perspective, had greater spiritual meaning than I could imagine (Isaiah 55:8-9).

This success being bestowed upon me was, in fact, the baptism of the Holy Spirit (Matthew 3:11-12). As I continued my regular activities, I prayed in the Spirit during times of prayer, but I didn't change anything about my life. I was focused on my responsibilities, attempting to balance it all: my children, at that time two grandchildren, the business, my job, my involvement in Church and recovery functions, and lastly, taking care of myself.

In 2007, while exercising at the gym with a friend, I received a call that my father had collapsed after coming in from work and was en route to the hospital via ambulance. My friend and I left immediately for the hospital. When we arrived, my father had been rushed into emergency surgery. My stepmom greeted us in the waiting room, gripped with fear. She explained what had happened and that she was really unsure what was wrong, that she was waiting for someone to come out and give us an update, but it was serious. So, we contacted family and waited, for what seemed like an eternity.

After many hours, a nurse came out to inform us that we could go up to a waiting room outside of the neurological ICU for brain injuries. She stated we would have to ask the doctors for more information. It wasn't until this communication that we gained some idea about what was even wrong with my dad. Finally, sometime in the middle of the night, a team of doctors wheeled my father out of surgery on a stretcher. At the sight of him, I literally collapsed in a heap on the floor, sobbing. I never knew a human head could become so swollen; my father was unrecognizable. All I remembered hearing the doctors say was, "We've done all we can to save him; it's now up to God whether he makes it through the night." They proceeded to wheel him into the ICU, informing us that only one of us would be permitted to visit him once every hour for 15 minutes, beginning the next hour, because they needed time to get him settled in the intensive care unit and on life support systems as soon as possible.

After we all got past the initial shock, I went into the restroom and locked the door. I got down on my knees and began to talk to the Lord, weeping, "Lord, my mother is already with You; please don't allow my father to die if he is not in right standing with You." I realized years later that the Holy Spirit had led me to pray that specific prayer. I knew that my father had been angry with God, and though he was raised as a Christian, he had begun to explore other religions and attempted to lead me into them. I remembered at that moment telling my dad that I was not in need of this other religion he was exploring, that I didn't believe in Jesus because he, my mother, and other family members had raised me in Church, but I believed in Him because of my personal experiences with Him. Now, here I was, crying out from the depths of my heart, begging the Lord to raise him up from this brain aneurysm and massive stroke. All I could think of was that I'd been here before with my mother.

As the next hour approached, everyone decided to

allow my aunt to go in and see my dad first. She is a nurse and could give us a clearer understanding of his condition. It was almost dawn. I went in the next hour, and at the sight of him, I gasped. There was a steel mount surrounding his head to prevent it from moving, and tubes were inserted in every place one could imagine.

Of course, my father was in a coma. As tears rolled down my face, I held his hand and prayed. I told him he had always been the picture of health; he was always health-conscious, exercising, and eating healthy was a way of life for him. I knew he was strong. My father played semi-professional golf when I was growing up and managed a local golf course for many years; in fact, I grew up on that golf course. I told him I loved him and needed him to fight, as he had always taught me not to give up. After 15 minutes had passed, I returned to the waiting area where my family was gathering and speaking with a doctor. He informed us that my father had a cerebral hemorrhage and that they had to saw off a portion of his skull to get into his brain to stop the bleeding, which was why the mount was there. He explained that the swelling would go down, but after entering his brain, he suffered a massive stroke. The doctor said he was very ill, there might be brain damage, and we just didn't know yet. "We've done everything possible to save his life at this point. If he emerges from the coma, we will go from there."

I was in a battle between faith and fear, and once

again I felt powerless. It's hard to watch the man who has always been your hero be so helpless. I was not going to leave him there alone. He had always been there for me, whether I was right or wrong. After several days, my daughter came to relieve me and insisted that I go home, shower, and rest. "You need to go and see about your business; I will stay with grandpa." She knew that was the only way I would leave because in 2001, I went to my mother's home to pick her up and found her deceased.

The following morning, I went to my office to discover that I had missed an inspector who randomly stopped by to perform compliance inspections while I had been at the hospital with my dad for the past several days. The notice informed me that I was non-compliant due to the fact that the door of the business was locked during reported hours of operation. They would make another unannounced attempt, and if the doors were locked again, I would be shut down. Addressing this caused me to remain at the office for the remainder of the workday before returning to the hospital that evening. However, now I was faced with a dilemma; this business was my baby. By this time, I had resigned from my job, and this was my only source of income. But the fear of my father being alone so close to death consumed me. The unresolved trauma of discovering my mother deceased led me to decide that if my father were to pass away, he would not be alone. I decided my new schedule would be take my younger children to school, go to work, and spend the evenings in the waiting room, visiting every hour throughout the night, I would go home early in the morning and start all over again. This went on for six months while my dad lay in a coma, During this time, I became aware that all three of my daughters were pregnant. As you could imagine, I was an overwhelmed emotional wreck to say the least. I was most hurt by my youngest daughter; my other two daughters were older, but I didn't want my children to experience the pain of some of the choices I made in my younger life, that led to me being a single parent. This is why I worked so hard to provide better for them, I became shut down and was basically going through the motions, just trying to cope with all that I was faced with. I remember asking God, "Who else would this happen to?"I remember my prophetic proclamation, "To whom much is given, much I required." I was presented with an offer to help me with the business so that I could attend to my personal family affairs. I accepted this offer, believing that the motivation was a love offering, and I was initially relieved. At least one thing had been lifted off my plate, because the weight of it all was enormous (Matt 11:28-30). My company provided nutritional products to some of our patients who had been prescribed these items, and we always delivered them. I had never had a problem with any orders I had received from a patient's doctor; I understood that I was only filling a prescription. I am not a physician and was unaware that this product, though prescribed by a physician, was not covered by certain insurance companies, except for intravenous use, which my father was actually surviving on at the time. I couldn't have imagined the consequences that would come from making decisions while under extreme emotional stress.

All of my father's affairs needed attending to as well while he lay unconscious day after day. Not to mention, my oldest son was expecting his second child at this time, which was almost too much to bear. Here, in a matter of months, I went from having six children—two in college, three in high school, one in middle school—and two grandchildren, who all still needed support. Now, four more grandchildren were all to be born around the same time. God said to be fruitful and multiply the earth, but this was a hundred-fold harvest to say the least—twelve children ranging from young adults to four infants all at once. And all the different assistance they needed: cars, tuitions, sporting events, daycare, and doctor's appointments for the new moms, along with all the provisions required in raising children. Thank God, for the baptism of Holy Spirit; I am certain that it was the enabling grace of God that carried me through this time,as well as the increasing expenses of medical bills piling up over months of intensive care for my father.

CHAPTER 3

INTERCESSION

After months of essentially turning the hospital waiting room into a prayer/living area, my father regained consciousness. He was transported out of ICU into an observation unit. He had a tracheostomy and could not talk, but he was conscious, and he could move his eyes and squeeze my hand.

After being moved to this unit, he then contracted an infection and became critical once again. Requiring a full covering from neck down in order to visit him, he began to hallucinate due to this infection and high fever, and had to be restrained to the bed because he kept pulling out the many tubes. When I was allowed in to visit him, I always prayed with him and assured him that everything would be okay; I could see fear in his eyes. I knew what it was like to have many questions and not be able to verbalize them. Years later, my stepmom shared with me that during this time, my dad had written her a request asking her to inform the medical staff to remove the life support and just let him go on from this life. She saw the hopelessness in his eyes and said, "No, I will not. Please don't give up. Andrea has been almost living in this hospital; the only reason she's not here now is because I'm here. If she comes back here and you're gone, I'm not sure she can handle that. She has her Church and everyone praying for you. We love and need you; please don't give up."

Finally, my dad was stabilized and released to an intensive rehabilitation facility. The portion of his brain that had been affected was associated with motor skills; therefore, he was like a child again, unable to care for his basic needs such as eating, walking, and even talking effectively. So, the journey continued. During his time in rehab, I maintained my schedule of visiting my father faithfully. However, several weeks into the rehab, my father's medical team forbade me from continuing to spend the nights, informing me that my father would most likely need care indefinitely and that I needed to get some rest and prepare myself for the long-term care he would require. Because God had essentially performed a miracle already, right before my eyes, and I was exhausted, I took their advice and began going home at night.

One evening while visiting my father, my youngest daughter called me saying she was in labor. I rushed home to take her to the hospital, and the next morning, the first of these three babies arrived. After finally getting my daughter and the baby into a room, my middle daughter called, saying she was in labor. My oldest children rushed her to the same hospital, and here I was, going back and forth from one room to the labor room, attempting to be there for both daughters and their babies. The next day, the second baby and my first grandson arrived. Now I was in love with these two bundles of joy, born 48 hours apart. Thankfully, the third baby gave us a break and was born two months later—a baby girl. We were the talk of the hospital; everyone came to see these almost-twin cousins. As you can imagine, once the moms and babies were resting, I went home to shower and get some much-needed rest.

Here, my life's hurts were triggered. The next morning in prayer, I talked to the Lord about the fact that I didn't want my daughters to have to experience the things I did as a young mother. Unaware at this time in my life that prayer is a conversation between us and God, I would go to Him with my cares but thought that I should just do what I thought was right and believe He would direct the outcome. I prayed amidst not yet realizing that prayer is not complete until I receive God's guidance. I decided to buckle down and support them instead of forcing them into situations where they would be dependent on strangers, as I had experienced in my earlier years of being thrust into government assistance. Not understanding spiritual law, I vowed to never allow my children to face the difficulties that I had. I never wanted them to experience the shame, rejection, or abandonment that plagued me most of my life. Neither did I want them to be thrust into situations with people who didn't know their hearts or genuinely love them. Finally, the years of hard work had positioned me to have the means to provide a better life for us all. I decided that I would employ them and teach them how to operate the business to prepare them to take care of themselves and their children. This would give them skills to begin their life's journey with support from me. The motive of my heart was to teach them the business and expand; I love my children— for most of my life, they were the only family I really had.

After bringing the babies home, I was right back running around, trying to juggle all my hats, visiting my dad again and sharing with him that he had more great-grandchildren. My father wrote a note to me saying he was aware that I had been living in the waiting area and praying for him, and that when he felt like giving up, he held on because of me. As you can imagine, this touched my heart in a deep way. It was difficult to see my father so helpless. I think of the scripture, "We are once an adult and twice a child." I had felt so powerless to help him, so this letter really comforted me, and I had hope and faith that he would overcome. I would take care of him as he had taken care of me. Even in his condition, he was concerned about leaving me. What neither of us realized at the time was that the Lord was preparing us both to forgive and heal our relationship while answering my prayer, prayed in the hospital restroom many months before the night he first fell ill. Praise the Lord for His faithfulness!

Finally, my father was being released from the intense rehabilitation facility to a skilled nursing facility to continue rehab and stabilization. Now I was faced with a new dilemma. At that time, I lived in a home that had only one bedroom downstairs. As my father's medical team had informed me, we were preparing for his care upon release from this now third medical facility. As my family discussed his long-term care, I decided to move my whole life back to a side of town where I had previously lived while raising my children and where I had first opened the business. Because I was blessed to buy and build my own home, I was able to design it to my liking and to meet all of our needs: living quarters for my dad, my two daughters and their babies, as well as two sons that still resided with me. I moved the company to a location near the new home so that I would be close to the house in case a situation arose with my father.

After the completion of the home, we all transitioned and finally brought my father home to begin the next phase of care. He, of course, needed continued care;

therefore, I now needed a home health agency. How ironic that my grandmothers, mother, and I had previously worked as private duty caregivers. After several months of adjusting to my new life and figuring out how to fit my father's full-time care into my routine, I began to try and make sense of it all. I had to figure out my father's finances and his retirement, which he had resisted prior to falling ill. He had told me he wanted to work until he could no longer do so, or he wouldn't know what to do with himself. As I've mentioned, he loved the golf course. He told me as I was growing up to seek to do what I was passionate about; that way, I would never feel like it was work. He had demonstrated that throughout my life, always pursuing his interests. Now he was forced to retire and draw his pension, and I considered how difficult this had all been and would continue to be for my dad. I sought to include him in decisions about his life and to respect him as a man first and foremost, especially regarding his daily care, hygiene, and privacy. In this way, his grandsons were a great help, assisting him with the bathroom and such after the 24-hour care subsided.

I began to consider going back to work, so I had the alarm company come out and install a medical alert system for my father that he could wear around his neck. If he needed medical attention, he could just press the button, and the alarm system would call an ambulance and notify me at my office, which was ten minutes away.

Notice I had not mentioned anything about the business; I rarely went to the office during this time. Several times, needs arose that required my involvement, so I quickly resolved them, such as the need to purchase equipment or other medical products. Because I had been the sole owner, I was placed in a position to go to my banking institution and add another person to transact business so that the company could remain afloat. There were bills, salaries, purchase and shipping costs, deliveries, maintenance for company vehicles, and other expenses of daily operations. Prior to this time, I had maintained all of the responsibilities alone, with my sons delivering equipment on the weekends. Again, I never considered this to be an unwise decision because I naively believed that the people I placed in charge loved me and had my best interests at heart—not only mine but my whole family's.

As we began to gain some sense of normalcy, I slowly started incorporating activities back into my life. Because my father was angry about the quality of life he had to come to accept, it was sometimes difficult to care for him. I decided, at the advice of my spiritual mother, to begin taking care of myself. She suggested I go get my hair styled, get a massage, start going back to the gym, and, of course, maintain my mental and emotional health. "Go to work and take care of your business," she said. "You've taken care of everyone except yourself. God entrusted you with that company; go back and take care of your baby. You've done well with all that's been thrust upon you; please take care of yourself." Because she had walked with me for many years, I trusted her. I knew she was right, but because of my life experiences, I had been conditioned from childhood to become very skilled at taking care of everyone except myself; the role of rescuer was familiar. I would later learn that this was not the will of my Father in Heaven, that boundaries and balance are necessary to live a full life, and that it's okay to take care of ourselves. I had learned to neglect myself as a way of life. The Lord would later teach me that this behavior grieved His heart—the fact that God's children didn't realize our true worth and value or understand our true identities in Christ (Revelation 1:6; 1 Corinthians 6:19-20).

As I began to incorporate work and other activities back into my life, I started to feel some sense of relief. I got a new hairstyle, began working out, and enjoyed social events with friends. Around this time, I realized that the company had grown during my absence and seemed to be doing well. Because of my new short haircut, one of my sons suggested I go next door to a barber shop and have my hair edged up. I was apprehensive about going into a shop full of men, so I tried to contact my stylist first, but she was on vacation, and I had a speaking engagement, which is why I wanted my hair cleaned up. As the day of the engagement approached, I finally decided to go over to the barber shop and ask for the guy my son had suggested. These men all knew my children, but my only interaction with them had been simple greetings of "Hi, Mama T" out of respect. As I entered, the volume and conversations came to a screeching halt. All eyes were directed at the door and me, which is why I had attempted to avoid going there in the first place. One of the barbers, who I was familiar with, said, "Hey, Mama, is everything okay?" I responded, "Joe sent me here for Mr. Lark to cut my hair, please." He spoke up and said, "Yes, ma'am, have a seat." I had never seen this particular guy before, and as I sat quietly in the chair, he stated, "You can relax; I'm not going to mess up your hair." I guess he could sense how uncomfortable I was. He then asked how I knew Joe. I stated, "He is my son." "Oh," he said, "you are the owner of the equipment company next door. It's nice to meet you." "Likewise," I responded, and shortly after that, he said, "All done." I paid him and hurried to leave. As I turned to say goodbye and thanked everyone, I noticed he was handsome. After this, I began to see this man around, and we would speak in passing, but no more than just a "hi." Until one day, I was standing outside smoking a cigarette, and he initiated a conversation with me. We spoke briefly, and I returned to work.

Several months later, I stayed late one night at the office, working on an inquiry about an employee that was time-sensitive. It was also storming, and I was waiting for the rain to let up before getting into my truck. After a while, realizing the rain wasn't letting up, I decided to attempt to navigate my way home. As I walked out of my office and turned to lock the door, I noticed several people looking out of the front door of the complex, saying, "Oh no, it's flooded out there." About that time, the guy who had cut my hair emerged from the barber shop to see what the commotion was about. He was surprised to see me standing at the window with my purse and briefcase and asked if I had an umbrella. When I said no, he went back into the barber shop and got his. There was an older lady standing there before I came out to leave. He took her keys, went out, and drove her car up to the door, walking her to her car underneath his umbrella. He asked if she would drive me to my car, but the lady drove off. We both looked at her in shock and burst into laughter. He asked for my keys and brought my truck around to the door and walked me to the car. I thanked him and, smiling, asked if he needed a ride to his car since it was still raining. He assured me he would be fine and simply said, "Drive safe, goodnight."

Several weeks later, leaving the office one evening, I walked out, and he was standing outside. He asked if he could help me.Inside my car, I had a box of files as well as my purse and briefcase, so I allowed him to carry the box. He asked if I was married, and I replied, "No, I'm not." He went on to say, "I see you working hard and taking care of your business. Do you ever have any fun?" I paused and thought about his question, smiling as I said, "Yes, I do sometimes." He asked if he could take me out sometime, and I told him I would think about it and drove off. Honestly, I had not thought of dating in quite a while.

Weeks later, I saw him in passing, and he asked if he could walk me out at the end of the workday. I said yes, but as the time to leave approached, I became nervous and snuck out without him seeing me. Maybe I was running because he had expressed interest in me, and for many reasons, that scared me—none having to do with him, but past failed relationships had caused me to be apprehensive. I avoided him to escape the presumption of pain. When I saw him again, he joked, "Oh, you faked me out, huh? I came at 5 PM to walk you out, and you burned off on me. What's wrong? You changed your mind?" Before I knew it, I said my birthday was coming up, and I'd like to go to Tyler Perry's gospel play that's coming to town that weekend. "Okay, then, we will." A friend of mine, he, and I went to the play and out to eat for my birthday, and we had a nice time.

After this first date, I was less apprehensive. We began speaking and associating more frequently, and this dating evolved into a relationship. As time went on, he was integrated more and more into my life, which meant the lives of everyone in and around my life. I've learned from my own life experiences that we, as humans, often reject change initially, especially when someone we love is involved, believing we know what and who is best for another, lacking the faith to trust God in certain areas of our lives. This enmeshment, if not communicated through and boundaries established, can destroy relationships. The person attempting to protect believes they are moving out of love, but true love is freedom. The person being protected can feel resentful and be tempted to yield to a spirit of rebellion due to the perceived control, insinuation that they are incapable of making their own decisions, and loss of freedom to choose. I've learned how prideful it is to enforce our views, opinions, plans, and agendas on another. Without clear guidance from the Lord, leaning to our own understanding is dangerous and has caused much pain in this world (Proverbs 3:5-6).

My life became more balanced, and I began to enjoy my life as I sought to balance it all and include self-care into the equation; it seemed the storm was over. As the babies grew older, I began training my children on how to operate the business, teaching them how every department operated and observing their individual strengths and abilities to determine which area their skills would work best. This caused them to flourish and develop a personal skill set along with self-confidence and esteem. Having supervised facilities for others, I used those skills now to bless my business and family. I was able to hire and train a staff that placed me in a position to oversee and really focus on administrative duties. I attempted to be hands-on to assist in areas of uncertainty; I was not good at micromanaging, and this would prove to be my undoing.

Now the people I permitted to operate the company in my absence were asked to take a slight pay cut to expand the operation, with a promise to reinstate their salaries in six months to a year in order to establish a second location. I had shown complete trust in them and never neglected my obligations concerning their salaries or responsibilities, even in the midst of all that had befallen me. Therefore, I believed I could expect the same respect; however, this decision caused anger, resentment, and a loss of relationships that I couldn't have fathomed. This was only a temporary pay cut that would later ensure the return of salary with the possibility for an increase. I thought trusting that I would keep my word had clearly been displayed and established.I stood my ground and proceeded, believing that after careful consideration, things would work out for the best on all our behalf. The outcome was the total opposite; there was lots of relationships that deeply hurt me and left me bewildered. I prayed about this situation, and after speaking with several people, I decided that maybe God had allowed things to work out this way, as I really needed and appreciated the help during this pass very difficult season of life. Maybe this was His way of leading me and exposing truth that I was unaware of at the time. Though disappointed, I knew in my heart my motives were pure, so I carried on, stepping back into the daily operation as I had previously, now with a full staff in place that included all of my children except my youngest son, who was in barber college at the time. As we began to implement the expansion, things progressed, and of course, the responsibilities increased. However, the teamwork that had been a way of life for my children and I naturally took effect.

By 2010, the expansion was complete; we owned and operated a second location, both fully staffed. My father was stable and improving, the babies were growing, and their parents were able to provide for themselves. We were also able to provide employment to others and quality equipment and care for our patients. My significant other also helped out when needed. I was happy, and all was well, or so I thought. Because of my increasing need to be at work, I realized this left my father home with only his healthcare provider and little socialization. I decided to enroll him in an adult daycare program where he could regain some sort of activities. There, he would have peers to interact with and get out of the house several days a week. I signed him up part-time initially, as he had only been out for medical appointments, Church and dinner, which usually exhausted him. He enjoyed the center, attending three days a week. One day, while being transported to an outing, my father fell and hit his head on the pavement. They called me to inform me of the fall and that he was en route to the hospital. Here we go back to the medical center. I notified his doctor because they had taken him to another hospital. He agreed to meet us there. When we arrived, my father had a brain bleed and needed surgery. As you can imagine, I was very upset, having to see my father endure another surgery as well as the recovery process.

CHAPTER 4
ACTIVATION

He had come such a long way; the battle in my mind and emotions resurfaced, but this time my faith was stronger. God had brought him through before when even the best healthcare professionals wondered if it was possible. An extreme faith rose up in me, and I decreed that this time, while he was in surgery, God would do it again (1 Cor 12:9). I decided that this time, in the waiting room, I would shift the atmosphere and speak life over my dad, declaring that the doctors' hands, minds, and all their skills would come under the direction of the Lord Jesus Christ. I decreed that ministering angels were dispatched to the operating room, not only for him but for the entire hospital. So instead of falling to the floor, consumed with fear, I stood in faith. It wasn't until sometime later that I realized it was the Holy Spirit who had empowered me with this gift of faith and led me to pray the faith-filled words of life with authority. The Holy Spirit was rising up in me, and I wasn't even aware of His work in and through me at the time (1 Cor 12:11). Praise God for His faithfulness! Years prior, a dear friend of mine told me, "Once invited, God's will will be done in your life with or without your permission!" I didn't even realize I was being trained in intercessory prayer.

After the surgery was complete, we were informed that he had fallen headfirst, causing a new rupture. They went in and stopped the bleeding; however, because of the pre-existing injuries, they were unsure if he was strong enough to pull through. He was again in critical condition and in a coma. Here he was in ICU again; however, the desperate need to live in the waiting room was gone. At that time, I had an inner knowing that he would be okay. As before, I came to visit and pray over him daily, unaware I was learning how to bring every thought into the obedience of Christ (2 Cor 10:5). Because the enemy tried to condemn me with thoughts and accusations, such as, "It's all your fault. If you hadn't put him in the adult daycare program, he wouldn't have fallen," attempting to lure me into guilt, doubt, and self-condemnation. Instead of agreeing with his lies, I spoke out the truth, knowing my motives toward my father were pure and considerate of him. The Lord spoke to my heart during one of these mental battles. Very simply, He said he could have fallen anywhere, meaning even if I had not taken him to the daycare, he could have fallen at home. I knew this was the Lord and realized that the stranger's voice I should reject (John 10:1-5). The Lord later told me this: "Anything that doesn't agree with My Word, Will, and Way, you know it is not ME. Don't allow the enemy to do all the talking!"

My father again contracted an infection and high fever during his recovery. While sitting with him one evening, he was very ill and began hallucinating. Again, he was restrained to the bed for his own protection. He was attempting to get out of bed, asking who I was, stating his mother and my mother, who had both gone to be with the Lord, were there to get him. He was wrestling to get free of the restraints; this alarmed me, and the battle began. I went over to comfort him, laying my hands on him, saying, "I'm here, Dad. You are not alone; just try and rest. I'll be right here." As I did, he began to relax and eventually fell asleep. Of course, I remained there all night, praying and watching. Early in the morning, the Lord spoke these words to my heart: "This sickness is not unto death," reminding me that we have not been given a spirit of fear but of power, love, and a sound mind (2 Timothy 1:7). Therefore, I was freed to succumb again to living in the hospital out of fear. I now had a heart assurance that, despite how bad the situation looked in the natural, all was well. I could leave and live until I visited him the next day, knowing the Lord was with him. Surely, he began to improve daily, and once stable, back to the rehabilitation facility we went.

One day, as I walked into the office, the office manager informed me of a notice to providers of an upcoming audit of all healthcare providers in our region. She said, "I'll print out the notification letter and all the attachments and bring them to you. Also, I need to speak with you privately." "Very well," I responded, and proceeded to my office. A while later, she came to bring the information. I invited her to come in and have a seat. She gave me the documents and said, "I have something to tell you, and I'm not quite sure how to say it." I could see she was perplexed, which had never happened before. Because of her obvious apprehension, I assured her that she could talk to me about anything, then asked, "What's wrong?"

She began to share with me that she had a dream about me and had been undecided whether to tell me or pray for me. But because she couldn't decide, she had prayed and asked God for direction. She went on to say, "When you walked in, I knew I was supposed to tell you." "Okay, go ahead and tell me," I said. She began to share the dream and said, "But the part I feel that the Lord really wants me to tell you is that He says you will be more useful to Him without money." I could see her physically relaxed after she told me about the dream. She stated, "I will give you time to review the documents; just let me know what you need me to do." Now I was perplexed; so bewildered, I responded, "Okay, I'll let you know." As she exited, I asked her to close the door behind her, please.

Sitting there quietly for a while, I pondered the dream, trying to fathom what in the world it could mean. I even questioned whether this dream was from God, simply because of the Word from God through my daughter several years back that "success had been bestowed upon me." I also questioned why God would give the dream to her. I must admit my biased pride; I thought of her as a baby Christian who was not yet surrendered to Christ as Lord of her life, which caused me to receive the Word with skepticism. Lesson: God can use anything or anybody He chooses; He once spoke through a donkey!

Of course, my attention turned to the audit and preparation for it. I was surprised because, at that time, I had owned and operated this business for close to ten years and had never been audited before. However, since the notice stated all healthcare providers in our region, I assumed it was just a new regulation they were implementing. I read the information and informed the office manager to notify all employees of a mandatory staff meeting the following day to inform them that the government would be coming out to audit the company. We would perform an internal audit to ensure we were as prepared as possible and clarify everyone's responsibilities.

So we did. The following day, I ordered lunch for everyone and held the meeting at midday, knowing some had children and families to get home to. During this first meeting, every department was given a copy of the standards and requirements for their department and asked to begin an assessment to determine any deficiencies or materials needed to bring those weaknesses into compliance. We would meet weekly until every issue was resolved and then hire a medical auditing firm to come in and train us all in the new regulations and perform an in-house audit to ensure our success. During this process, I often thought of the dream and still questioned the meaning and source of it all. We all worked hard to complete the pre-audit plan by the deadline while maintaining the daily responsibilities of the business.

When the time arrived for the audit, we had completed the preparations. We had all been trained and received certifications of completion in each department regarding the new standards and passed the internal audit, which was pricey, I might add. Because everyone had worked so hard, I gave bonuses and treated them to dinner. Even my significant other assisted, and he did not work there. This act of appreciation would later be described as bribery, along with many other untrue accusations. This was the beginning of the end of that chapter of life for me, my family, and my employees, and it would later reveal that the dream indeed was from God. What a journey we were all about to take!

When the auditors actually came to carry out the inspection, we passed, and the company was given a certificate of completion. We all breathed a sigh of relief and continued on with work and life as usual. Remember that I said we carried on as usual. In the fall of 2010, two dear friends of mine passed away within several months of each other.

Of course, these losses deeply affected me, mainly because I had allowed disagreements to cause me to shut them out after over twenty years of friendship. I was never able to articulate a vow I had lived by for years until I heard James Jordan, founder of Father Heart Ministries along with his wife Denise, preach about the orphan heart. He said that, as a young child, I had made a decision that involvement with people was so painful that the less I associated with them, the less likely I was to be hurt. This was the essence of his statement. When I heard it, it was a profound awakening. I realized that I, too, had come into agreement with the enemy of our souls, believing this lie. I hadn't recognized that the agenda behind this assignment was to isolate, inflict loneliness, invoke fear, create a lack of trust, and ultimately lead one into spiritual imprisonment.

Mr. Jordan went on to say that true loneliness isn't about knowing people, but rather the fact that no one really knows us. Years earlier, I had heard clients express, while counseling, that they could be surrounded by people and still feel alone. Despite having heard that statement before, I never truly understood it until that meeting that day. The reality that God was speaking to me through His son—and the anointing on him—opened the ears of my understanding and began the process of deliverance from the spiritual bondage I had lived in for many years. I share all this to explain why I shut these dear friends out; hurt and disappointment caused me to withdraw.

During this time, they both passed away, and these events plunged me into profound pain, leaving me unaware of the root cause of this grief. I had not yet come into the previous revelation. Regret overwhelmed me, and I entered a mental battle of "could have" and "should have" called them, forgiven them, and resolved our differences. The stark, disappointing reality that reconciliation was now impossible devastated me because, in truth, despite my attempts to protect myself from future hurt by distancing myself from these individuals, I genuinely loved them both.

CHAPTER 5

THE APPOINTED TIME

Several months later, I received an invitation to speak in Dallas, Texas, on the topic of grief and the recovery process. As I was navigating the grief process myself, I accepted the offer. The convention was scheduled for the weekend after Thanksgiving in 2010. After spending the holiday with family and friends, several of us packed up and headed to Dallas for the event. I spoke that Saturday. As I made my way down from the podium, an older lady approached me, asking to speak privately. Because I did not know her, I assumed she wanted to discuss grief. Stepping away from the crowd to talk with her, she said, with intense conviction, that the whole time I had been speaking, the Lord kept telling her, "She is a preacher; she is a teacher."

I was shocked by her statement. However, seeing her seriousness, I replied, "Oh no, ma'am, I am not a preacher. This is my ministry; I hope something I shared helped you, but essentially, I am too sinful to be a preacher. I am a Christian, and I love the Lord very much." But she was persistent: "No, no, no, the Lord says you are a preacher." As I longed to step outside for a cigarette, and she would not relent, I finally responded, "Ma'am, God Himself will have to tell me that." I hugged her and walked away.

While standing in the smoking area, I pondered this encounter and found it unbelievable. Honestly, I even questioned the lady's sanity, not realizing that my reality—or lack thereof—was about to be shattered! I then asked everyone present while I spoke if they saw this older lady who had pursued me, but none of them claimed to have seen her. I went outside to the smoking area where she had followed me, and still no one had seen her. I just couldn't figure this encounter out (Hebrews 13:2).

The following weekend, while sitting in a salon having my hair styled and casually reading a book, I was approached by yet another older lady. Because I didn't know this lady, I assumed she was speaking to the stylist, so I continued reading. The young lady who was doing my hair said to me, "Ms. T, this lady is speaking to you." As I raised my head and turned toward the lady, I responded, "Oh, ma'am, I'm sorry, I didn't realize you were speaking to me. I apologize for not paying attention to what you were saying." Before I could ask her to repeat herself, she said, "I have a word from the Lord for you; will you receive it?" I was stunned, but because she was an older woman and her facial expression was matter-of-fact, I said, "Yes, ma'am, I will."

She began by saying, "The Lord says to stop running from Him." I became defensive in my mind, thinking, "I'm not running from the Lord; I love the Lord. I attend Church faithfully, pay my tithes, and help anyone I can within my ability to do so." Of course, all these truths were related to external help and my religious façade. She continued, "He says to stop rejecting the women who are coming to you for help; it is Him that's leading these women to you." This statement pierced my heart because I had no defense for it. She went on to say, "The Lord says He wants you to lead the man you are involved with back to Him; He placed you in this man's life for His glory." This also shook me because how could she know that I was involved with a man? Almost trembling, I asked her, "Can you ask the Lord why He says I am running from Him? Because I'm not running from Him intentionally, and I'm feeling sadness in my heart because I have truly sought to know the Lord." She went on to say that the Lord says, "The Holy Spirit is going to visit you, and at that time, you will know with crystal clarity why you were sent to earth!" She then asked if it was okay for her to lay her hand on me and pray. "Yes, ma'am," I whispered. As she prayed and closed her prayer, I didn't realize just yet that she was releasing an impartation upon me. She turned to say goodbye to everyone and walked out of the salon. My first thought was that the stylist had told her all my business. Then I realized this young lady had not styled my hair in years; she couldn't have known these exact details of my life. I turned to ask who that lady was, and the stylist casually said, "Oh, she's a missionary from the Church down the street. She comes in regularly on Saturdays to have her hair done for Church when she is in town."

When I was a child, my grandmother and I went to the salon every Saturday to have our hair done for Church on Sundays as well, and my grandmother was the head of the mission board at the Church I was raised. Like the Samaritan woman at the well, only God could know every detail of my personal life (John 4:29-30). I asked for a minute and walked outside to smoke a cigarette, pacing up and down the walkway. The fear of the Lord fell on me, and I called my loved ones to explain all that the lady had said. My significant other reminded me of the lady who had approached me the previous week in Dallas, and he encouraged me to calm down and go back into the salon. "We will talk about it over dinner," he said, and so we did. I told him what the lady had said about him and led him in prayer.

For the next few nights, I stayed up most of the night, anticipating what would happen when the Holy Spirit came. All I had to reference were my two previous encounters with Him, so I was somewhat nervous. After several days, exhaustion forced me to sleep, as I also had to attend to all my responsibilities. As time went on, I began to prepare for the Christmas holiday. At that time, I loved to celebrate Christmas: the music, decorating, shopping, good food, family and friends, and most of all, I loved the Lord. Before I knew it, New Year's was approaching, and the Holy Spirit had not come. Family kept asking me about His coming due to their observation of the previous visitation. As we celebrated, I just said, "No, He has not come yet." My son said, "I have no doubt that we will all know when He comes."

New Year's passed, and we began the new year with life as usual: work and family Church attendance, of course. Because the words spoken to me in these two encounters had been the Words of God, they were alive and quick; they pierced me to my very heart and soul (Hebrews 4:12). I could not escape them. Though I continued with my normal responsibilities, they stayed on my mind continuously.

On January 10, 2011, He came. I was awakened at 5 a.m. by His voice. Before I attempt to put His voice into words, let me just say that in the previous encounters, I had first been slain in the Spirit, and the second time, I had gone up at Church to receive prayer for the baptism of His Spirit, and He rose up from within me. I experienced the Holy Spirit in a physically tangible way during those events, but this time, He spoke. In the book of Revelation 1:10, the Apostle John describes being encountered by the Holy Spirit and says he heard a great voice behind him, "like the calling of a war trumpet." Because I have never heard a war trumpet, I will describe it the best way I can: I heard a voice behind me that was like "thunder speaking." I sat up from a deep sleep and slowly turned to look behind me, but only the headboard and wall were visible. This voice permeated every fiber of my being, and I was terrified. I jumped out of bed, ran around turning on every light in the house, and began waking everyone up, asking, "Did you hear the voice calling me?" As they all replied no, some said, "Maybe you are dreaming; just go back to bed." I was almost incensed because this voice was all-encompassing. I said to my significant other, my father, and my sons, "I know everyone in Texas can hear this voice." But they looked at me like I was crazy, rolled over, and went back to sleep.

Their suggestion to go back to sleep was virtually impossible. When God speaks to you, the reality of frail humanity is clearly magnified. All prideful deception of one's self is shattered in an instant; intuitively Omnipresence was unveiled. Eventually, I made some coffee and proceeded to my prayer closet in the garage, so I could smoke several cigarettes and try to determine if I was dreaming. However, the fear of the Lord had come upon me again. Though I didn't yet realize what was going on at the core of my being, I knew it wasn't a dream. A friend called, unaware of the morning's events, saying she was on her way to town to handle some business and wanted to know if I would be available to meet her for lunch. Years before, on the way home from a speaking engagement in this sister's town, I had been told I was a preacher, and of course, I laughed it off, not realizing it was a prophetic word being spoken over me. I immediately told her to come and pick me up, that I was not going to the office, and would go with her downtown for lunch. I hurried in, got dressed, and anxiously awaited her arrival, pacing the floor. When she arrived, I jumped in the car with her, and we spent the day together before returning that evening as she prepared to drive back home.

I never mentioned to her the thunderous voice that had awakened me that morning. I went in, prepared dinner, and busied myself until bedtime. As I showered that night, pondering this voice, I instantly realized I had been running from God all day. What the Lord had led the woman at the salon to tell me about running from Him was true. Recall I said that this was the only thing the lady had said to me that I had an argument with. I repented, saying, "Lord, I am so sorry for running from You. You know that I love You; please forgive me." I felt an overwhelming peace come over me at that moment.

The next morning, the Holy Spirit called me again at 5 a.m., and I jumped up looking around. Still, I could only hear His voice; I jumped out of bed again and went into the kitchen to make coffee. I thought, I don't know how not to run. I went out to the garage just to be with the

Lord and ask, "What is going on, Lord?" I continued the same anxious behavior that day, though I was keenly aware of it. I began cleaning the house almost obsessively as the guys all headed out for work. I could see by their facial expressions that they were concerned for me. One by one, they asked, "Are you coming to work? Why are you cleaning the house? Did you fire the housekeeper? Are you sure you are okay?" I responded "no" to all three questions. It happened again: this thunderous voice woke me up again this morning at 5 a.m., calling my name.

If they were bewildered, try to imagine how I felt. I was too afraid to even respond "yes" to the Lord. All I knew was that I felt like my every thought, action, and being were under a microscope. Omniscience was there in the house. I remember thinking, the last time the Holy Spirit came, we lived at a different address. The reality that He truly knows everything was real to me for the first time. Though I knew this scripture in my head, I was now actually experiencing it in my heart and house. Questions flooded my mind: He actually knows my name, He obviously knows everybody who is in this house, He knows all my sins, yet I feel totally loved and aware that He is mindful of us. I wondered what the purpose of His calling was. What was the significance of Him coming the past two mornings at exactly 5 a.m.? Almighty God wants to talk to me, of all the people on earth? Who else is this happening to? Do I just talk to Him like I do when I'm praying, or is it inappropriate to speak to a Holy God? Should I speak in tongues or English? Why can't anyone else hear Him? Have I sinned too much? What in the world is going on? It was as if He stood near, observing every question of my mind and heart, yet did not respond, which made His presence more frightening. Reading Psalms 139 and experiencing it are different, as the scripture says in Isaiah 55:8-9.

I decided to stay in the house all day, which was my attempt to show the Lord that He had my attention and I would not run from Him any longer. I went in to sit with my dad and talk to him about these events. As I sat there silently pondering it all, my father eventually asked me what was wrong. Because I didn't quite know how to respond, I blurted out, "God is calling me." He turned to look at me and simply said, "Answer Him." It was as if a light bulb turned on in me; I thought to myself, You act like this is a minuscule event. After sitting there quietly for a while in this inward battle, I got up and busied myself in the house with cooking and cleaning, clearly aware that I was, to some degree, afraid of the One I so deeply loved and had sought after for so long. I guess I believed you could not actually hear God until you died—not audibly, anyway. Because I had not yet realized that God had, in fact, been speaking to me all my life, through people and through the inward promptings of the Holy Spirit, I didn't know anyone personally who actually heard the voice of God except, obviously, for the two women who He spoke to me through recently.

Suddenly, I realized that what the lady in the salon told me was happening—that I was sent to earth for a purpose—was the reason for the visitation. This was beyond my comprehension. All my life, I had questioned why certain events happened to me and my family. I had always compared my childhood to others and, at times, been angry that I had to experience and live through some very difficult situations—some at no fault of mine and others were absolutely due to my sins and poor choices. Though I loved Jesus dearly, I had no framework for the Holy Spirit, and I probably feared Father God. I had no idea at that time that being in a relationship with the Lord was the catalyst to coming to know Father God. I only had the relationship with my earthly father to compare, and I was not really interested in another father due to some painful life experiences. I then projected this image of a father onto Father God. Also, in Baptist Church I had observed people shouting or becoming out of control, and I was told this was the Holy Spirit. As a child, that always scared me. Watching people flail around, run around, shaking, and passing out was unappealing to me, so I was also afraid of the Holy Spirit.

Though I had these previous experiences with the Holy Spirit, my fears of Him remained. My experiences of people in Church catching the Holy Ghost led me to think, But I am not at Church this keeps happening at home, and this time I was asleep. Thank God for His wisdom; He manifests Himself to each of us in a way He knows we can receive Him. I did not realize that the promise in John 14:20-23, 26 "Thy kingdom come, in Earth as it is in Heaven" was really possible.

I stayed up late that night watching Christian television, trying to figure out what was happening with all this. All I knew was that this was a life-changing event that I was experiencing alone, even in the midst of those I loved so much. They could not hear or see what was happening inside of me, which was a great source of frustration. I thought they must know I wouldn't lie about something like this; they all know how much I love the Lord. Especially my children—they have seen me worship and pursue a relationship with the Lord for years, privately, not just in Church attendance. Finally, I fell asleep with the TV on.

The third morning, I was awakened at 5 a.m. again by the Holy Spirit calling me. I jumped up and looked around, and my partner was sound asleep. Joyce Meyer was on the TV teaching. When I turned to get out of bed, I was confronted by the person of the Holy Spirit. An invisible person was standing there; the power was indescribable. I fell to my knees in a heap, weeping, saying, "Lord, You know how much I love You; I don't know what it is You want me to do. I don't want to let You down. I smoke; I am living with this man I'm not married to. I love him, but I think I'm afraid to get married, and I occasionally use profane language."

My attention was drawn to the TV. I blurted out, "Oh,

I can't do that! I could never stand in front of that many people and speak." He then spoke, "We know everything about you. It's already been decided; those are issues of your flesh. We will work them out; we know your heart." I responded, "You want me to be a pastor?" In my mind, I thought of the preachers I've grown up listening to. He said, "No, an evangelist like Joyce. The Lord sent Me to anoint you for deliverance." "What is deliverance?" I responded. "I don't even know what that is! How can I do it?" "We will teach you," He said. "What is your answer?" The song "I Can Only Imagine" is the only way I can describe it; you can't imagine when love comes. As I lay there, undone on the floor, it was as if He stood there awaiting my answer. Running was impossible; I couldn't get around Him. Every time He spoke, every molecule in my body knew He was Elohim, the Creator God.

I finally said, "OK, yes Lord, I will do whatever it is You are asking, though I can't fathom why You want me; I feel so incapable." He said, "That is why We want you, because you know you can't do it without Us!" Then, instantly, it seemed He was gone, from standing there. Even now, as I write this, I struggle to explain the Holy Spirit. He is all power in a person; it was like a person standing in front of you who supersedes every human limitation, beyond natural senses. However, you can feel Him and hear Him. He is Resurrection Power walking and talking. I now know why Scripture records that you couldn't see Him and live. Earth has no comparison.

As I realized He had moved, I climbed up to sit on the bed to regain my composure; my knees were weak. I went to make coffee and went out to the garage to call into the prayer line of the friend who had come to visit a few days before. Mind you, I had not spoken of these events to her or anyone outside my immediate family. Before calling the prayer line, I remember pacing back and forth in the garage, so nervous and scared to smoke, then remembering Him saying, "We know everything about you." I said, "Lord, I need You to help me. I will do anything You ask, but I need Your help." Instantly, He said, "Don't allow your love for your children and father to prevent you from doing what I ask of you." Not understanding what that really meant, I said, "Oh Lord, I want to." Then I sat down and called the prayer line.

The host of this ministry began the meeting with the prayer agenda for the day, describing a family member's medical condition and asking for unified prayer concerning this. As soon as she finished speaking, surprisingly, I was transported in the Spirit (wrapped in His power) to another town where this lady was hospitalized, and I was standing in her room. She was gravely ill. Suddenly, I could see inside her body, and the Lord said to me, "This is what cancer looks like." What I saw was a black-greenish substance that appeared to be bubbling inside of her stomach; in the natural, it would look something like motor oil being boiled. As I observed this substance, the Lord went on to say, "Unforgiveness has opened many up to this destroyer." Suddenly, I was back in my garage, sitting in the chair on the phone. He then instructed me to tell the host that this lady was in need of a miracle, to go and tell her that if she would forgive, He would heal her. So, I did, and when I said these words, the host burst into tears, accepting the assignment. Later, I was told the source of this unforgiveness by my friend. She went that very day to visit this lady and delivered the Word from the Lord. Sadly, she succumbed to this spirit of infirmity and went home to be with the Lord.

Then the next woman began to express her prayer need on the call. As I listened, again I was rapt in His Spirit and transported to a prison. It was as if I was being suspended in the air, looking down into this prison—only in the spirit realm, though. I could not see any flesh, but I knew intuitively that there were many men in this prison, in many different inward and spiritual conditions. However, in this particular transport, the overwhelming demonic activity present and operating there was the purpose of this revelation. Unlike the previous transport, this one was vile and depraved. I was shocked to see these things in the spirit realm, and as I reluctantly looked on, the Lord spoke these words: "Prison is like hell on earth; it is one location where many demonic spirits are in operation." Suddenly, I was back in my chair in the garage, and the Lord instructed me to give a word to this lady as well. However, due to the sensitive nature of this word, I won't reveal it here. As I spoke these words to her, the same thing occurred—she began to weep. This instruction resulted in not only her but her whole family being delivered. Today, her life has been restored. Praise God! I'm so grateful to have been privileged to witness the delivering power of our Lord. It is true that God can use anything or anyone to accomplish His will, because I surely didn't have a clue what was going on. I simply observed what He showed me and said what He instructed me to say.

As the next lady began to share her prayer request, suddenly, a supernatural power manifested next to me. I must say I was so terrified that I was afraid to turn and look. In an instant, I was kicked up and placed on the ground; it felt as if I were like a feather to this being. The chair went one way, and the cigarette another. The women on the prayer line heard this and asked if everything was okay. I said, "Please don't hang up; I'm afraid." I don't know how long I had been down on the ground in the garage, but my fear was dissolved by the love in which I was submerged. However, it must have been several hours because eventually, one of my sons came to open the door. When he discovered me, as you can imagine, the expression on his face was alarm. He asked, "What happened? Are you okay?" Then he said, "Let me pick you up and bring you in on the rug in front of the fireplace; Mama, it's 30 degrees out here." But I responded, "No, don't touch me; they are doing surgery on me." He asked, "Who?" Then he asked, "Aren't you cold?" My response was, "No, I feel like I'm swimming in hot fudge or something; fire is literally coursing through my bones." With a look of utter disbelief, he slowly closed the door. Hours later, to this day, I still don't know how long I was down on the ground. I only know I went into the garage sometime close to 6 a.m. because that's when the prayer call began, and I didn't emerge from there until late afternoon. In these encounters, time seemed to be nonexistent; there is only a Now presence; there is no consciousness of before or after; natural time stands still. Matthew 3:11 is what I believe occurred that day. I had asked the Lord that morning to empower me to do what He asked. He told me to develop a relationship with the Holy Spirit.

After that morning, the eyes and ears of my understanding were enlightened. I didn't know it at the time, but I had just been enrolled in the school of the supernatural. The volume was turned all the way up, and I had 20/20 vision into what the Bible says: the spirit is more real than the natural. What an education I was in for! This began the teaching part of my journey into my purpose and destiny—the why I was sent to earth. Every morning at 5 a.m., the Holy Spirit woke me up for school. After several days, I became increasingly more comfortable with this overwhelming new reality. I began to get up, make coffee, and gather my Bible, pen, and paper to sit at the table prepared for class. He spoke to me audibly for a year and visually as well. Every day there was a new topic and lesson. I will highlight some of these lessons and how this all played out amidst what had been my daily life.

Early on, one day while in school, I was led into my dad's room by the Spirit and was flung to the floor in holy laughter. I was rolling around in unspeakable joy for no apparent reason, as though I was being tickled. My father raised up, looked down at me, and said, "Girl, there's something on you, like fire radiating from you." Then, his conscience was enlightened all of a sudden; he began recalling and telling me things he never had before. "Like when you were a baby, and your mother and I took you to Church to be christened; an old lady came up and decreed, 'This baby will be a prophet to the nations.'" In utter amazement, I asked, "Why was I never told this in 40 years?" He also said, "I believe the Lord called me, but I ran from Him." WOW! The veiled condition described in (John 12:40) was shattered by the glory of God, and joy ushered it in. The joy of the Lord is truly our strength.

One day during class, the Holy Spirit instructed me to ask Father God to heal me. My immediate thought was, "I'm not sick." But of course, I did what He said, again not having a clue as to what this meant. This healing began throughout that year and became more intense the following year. Thank God it continues throughout our lives as we yield, inviting the Father to heal our hearts, sin-sick souls, and minds. (Isaiah 60:1-4) is the will of God for humanity. A healed life preaches the greatest sermon, requiring few words. Hurt people hurt people. This I know well; I've been trespassed against, and I've equally trespassed against others. The mandate to the body of Christ is to be healed people who present healing to others. In class this day, the Holy Spirit gave me a vision of thousands of Christians sitting in Church with nooses around their necks, bound by life's painful circumstances. In this vision, our Lord was deeply saddened as He beheld His bride. I still hadn't realized that this was my condition, which is why the Holy Spirit said I needed to be healed. I had sought to be healed in many different ways. I learned, however, that you can't heal a spiritual malady with a natural solution.

One day, during class, several of my children came to the house to speak with me out of concern.Tthey said, "Mom, first we are glad you haven't smoked in months," which I had not even paid any attention to. My response was, "ThankGod." They went on to list their concerns, saying things like,"You've not come to your own business, you haven't hadyour hair done, and you haven't gone anywhere else except to Church.All you do is sit in this house and write and read the bible every day. This has been going on for 5 months." We are not going to the store for you anymore to purchase groceries or tablets, and we have things that require your signature and attention at the office." My response to them was, "None of those things compare to being in the presence of the Lord. I've sought after this for years; I won't be moved. Bring the checks or whatever it is around here, and I'll sign them. I'll just go to the store and buy in bulk, and I will be fine."

They were shocked as they got up to leave. I hugged one of my daughters, who was the last to walk out of the house, and she was slain in the Spirit, falling to the floor and lying there for several hours. When my daughter came to, she said, "There was fire all over me." When I waved my hand to alert my other daughters that my youngest daughter had fallen under the power of the Holy Spirit, they also said a wave of glory hit them. They all said, "Mama, we can't stay here all day passed out under the power of the Holy Spirit. Somebody's got to operate the business." Smiling, I agreed because, for me, there was no other option.

As previously mentioned, healing had begun. One morning, I awoke at 5 a.m. and began my daily class schedule. As I made coffee, the Lord asked me a question. I've learned that when the Lord asks a question, it's not because He is unaware of the answer; His desire is to shatter the veil of deception and reveal the truth. "And you shall know the truth, and the truth shall make you free." (John 8:32).

He simply asked me if I believed the Word (the Bible), which is Him (John 1:14), and the Word became flesh, or did I only attend Church because that's what I had traditionally been taught to do? To say I was stunned is an understatement. I knew He was observing my every thought. I had to sit down and truly ponder His question for what seemed like quite a while. I felt like a child who had misbehaved, being questioned by my father while knowing I was guilty. Sheepishly, I almost whispered, "No, Lord, I believe you."

He then said, "If you believe Me, why have you allowed the enemy to torment you so long over Rita?" I couldn't have imagined this being the reason for the initial question. My response was, "Lord, I was just so hurt that my mother died there in her home alone. I hoped all my life that You would heal her." The realization of that hope being unfulfilled plunged me into a despair I had not known.

What I failed to disclose in this writing is that I found my mother deceased in her home ten years previously, and I had not even realized that it was Satan who had assaulted me mentally, emotionally, and physically. My constant thought was, "I should have gone earlier when she didn't answer the phone. Maybe I could have gotten her to the hospital. She was there all alone, just breaking my heart." I plunged into pain and sadness so deep I couldn't get out of it.

Eventually, I went to the doctor and, in tears, explained the situation and my inability to function. I was prescribed antidepressants and anxiety medications. Over that decade, I had even gone to a psychiatrist seeking help for the deep trauma I experienced related to my mother's illness as well as her death. I had also attended twelve-step programs, of which I had actively been a member for 18 years at that time. I had no choice but to find a way to go on; my heart remained broken.

This morning's lesson led me back to my bed to lie down, perplexed, which I had not done in months. The Holy Spirit had routed a daily schedule in me; I got up at 5 a.m. and was in bed by 10 p.m. every day. Everyone who knows me knew that, in itself, was a supernatural accomplishment because I am not, by nature, a morning person. My son said, "Only God could wake Mom up at 5 a.m. and have her be so happy."

As I lay on the bed, by lunchtime, two of my daughters, along with one of their friends, stopped by to bring lunch for me and my dad. They came into my room asking why I wasn't in my now-normal position at the table, writing and studying. As soon as I finished explaining the morning's events, realizing that the Lord orchestrated this divine appointment, the Lord spoke and said, "Rita didn't die; I came and got her." My mother had been rushed to the hospital months before, dead on arrival, and was resuscitated.

He went on to say, "She asked to come back to say goodbye to prevent you from falling into the very snare that you succumbed to." What He meant was that during this hospitalization, my mother said to me, "I don't care what anyone else does; you continue with the Lord. You know the Lord." I didn't realize at that time she was really saying goodbye.

He said, "She asked to come home," and suddenly I was wrapped in the power of the Holy Spirit and lifted in a vision to heaven, standing before my mother. Like a child, I said, "Mama," and my heart was simultaneously healed. In this vision, my mother appeared to be about 20 years old—she was beautiful—and even asked me how my father and children were. I responded, "They're fine; Daddy's here, and the girls are right here."

Suddenly, my attention was turned to a river flowing behind my mother, and this water was alive; it was the only way I can explain it—it was living. This was the water Jesus promised the Samaritan woman in John 4:13-15.

He went on to say, "To be absent from the body is to be present with Me, I in you and you in Me." Suddenly, I was back in my room with these girls crying, saying, "Mama, we thought you died until you began to speak." The manifest presence of the Lord filled the room as we all were being healed; we wept. I ecstatically proclaimed, "I saw Mama! She is not dead, and she knew me; she even remembered you all! She is healed; she looked nothing like we last saw her here on earth." I erupted in unspeakable joy and ran to tell my father, who too had been deeply hurt by my mother's plight and passing.

This revelation has changed my reality; of course, Jesus has the keys of Hades and of death (Revelation

1:18). What Christ accomplished on behalf of humanity at the cross of Calvary was made clear, and the previous despair I carried over my mother's passing dissolved in the Truth. The Lord was so gracious to allow me to see that He has healed and delivered her. He went on to teach me the why and what of deliverance and the ravages of trespasses that have wounded the hearts of so many, requiring their healing.

When I inquired why this befell my mother and family, He simply said, "Though painful, you've been prepared; your mother was called to deliverance as well. However, she was not able to overcome; therefore, the mantle has been passed to you." Righteous indignation then rose up in me. I said to the Lord, "Teach me and use me to set as many free as possible from the snares of the enemy that so plundered my family."

Several days of teaching by the Holy Spirit concerning dying as a Christian, God's planned purpose and destiny for every soul created—this would be a book in itself—and time for me to digest it all. So many layers of deception fell away from my understanding, causing me to love the Lord so much more, as He first loved me and was mindful of my pain and bondage. He again delivered me so preciously; He is the lover of our souls. He died that we might actually live free indeed.

Next, in response to the Word at the hair salon to stop rejecting the ladies that come to me for help because the Lord is leading these women to you, rapt in the power of the Holy Spirit, I received a vision that addressed the reasons behind this command, as well as the root cause in me that led to why I had practiced this behavior.

This particular morning, as usual, I was awakened at 5 a.m., full of joy. I gathered my books, made coffee, and sat at the table prepared for the day's lesson when, all of a sudden, I was with the Lord in hell. I will attempt to reveal what I experienced. The Lord and I were elevated in the air over the lake of fire; pure evil and fear filled the atmosphere. The smell was a sulfuric stench, and the screeching cries of torment surrounded me. The absence of joy, peace, love, hope, grace, forgiveness, change, happiness, and righteousness—any good—did not exist there.

Though I didn't see anyone, I could hear people calling my name, begging for escape, allowing me to know they had memory of life and people they knew on earth, recognizing who I was. What I heard, smelled, and felt broke my heart; life's pain, despair, and hopelessness are no comparison. I observed the Lord weeping as well. Though this must have occurred in a short period of time, it seemed to be an eternity that we hovered in the air there. It was pitch black; the only way I was able to observe this flowing lake of fire was the glory that illuminated from the Lord.

I begged the Lord not to leave me there. What a sad place to be eternally! Suddenly, I was back in my kitchen, seated at the table, devastated. I sat there for a moment in sheer terror. I thought I knew terror prior to this experience, but I was wrong. I thought I understood God's love for humanity through Jesus' sacrifice on the cross; after this, I saw what He offered escape from, by way of the free gift of salvation. What greater love could one give than to lay down His life for another? What an insidious scheme to deceive people into this pit called hell. I felt physically sick; all I could do was cry. I realized the Holy Spirit knew I could bear no more that day. I went to lay down and wept for days after this.

It took me several days to ask the Lord why He took me there. Would He please go and get them out of there, I asked? How did they know my name? Who could I have known bad enough to go there? How tormenting it must have been to know the Lord was there yet did not rescue them. The sadness I felt over this was overwhelming. The Lord lovingly said, "I revealed this to you so that you understand the significance of what I've called you to do, that you don't quit when it becomes difficult." He then said, "I cannot take them out; this is fixed. One must decide before leaving earth. I will save a soul up until its last breath," He said. "I did not create this place for those made in My own image; it was created for Satan and his cohorts. However, many are there, and many will go there because they have been deceived into rejecting the free gift of salvation."

Intuitively, 1 Corinthians 6:9-20 was downloaded into my mind. I also knew who some of these souls were;

Revelation 12:7-9 was also downloaded into my mind. I cried, "Lord, these were not bad people." He said, "I do not make mistakes; they were deceived and failed to repent."

"Repentance is tripartite," He said, "not only admitting one's disobedience and asking for and receiving forgiveness, but changing of one's mind and the resulting actions is true repentance at a heart level. Man looks on the outward appearance; I look at one's heart." (1 Samuel 16:7) I realized intuitively that the Lord sees if someone has a change of heart literally.

The Holy Spirit taught me for the remainder of that week out of this revelation, using many verses of the Bible to illustrate this vision. He also led me through much deliverance concerning the theft of my true identity in Christ, addressing root causes as to why I had been rejecting the women that previously asked for my assistance to walk with them as they recovered. He exposed many erroneous beliefs I held about myself and others and how these beliefs hindered me, as well as robbed those the Lord wanted to touch through me.

To anyone reading this book, please accept the free gift of salvation, by simply praying this prayer: "Father, I know I am a sinner, I thank you for sending Jesus Christ to pay for my sins. Today, I accept the free gift of salvation by inviting You, Jesus, to come into my heart and life as the Lord of my life.Please save me and fill me with Your Holy Spirit. Order my steps lead me into the purpose and destiny for which I was created.Tthank You, Lord, for saving my soul, Amen.

Another memorable lesson involved a young lady who was associated with one of my sons. One day, she came to the house and asked if I would pray for her grandmother, who was hospitalized and very ill. She began to tell me how her grandmother had been such a sweet lady when she was a child and how she dearly loved her. However, over time, the grandmother became very hostile and unpleasant. As we discussed the changes in her grandmother's character, I asked her if she was aware of any hurtful events that might have caused this change. She felt it was a gradual decline that started after her grandmother began working in the prison system. Instantly, I recalled the vision I had about the prison.

As we began to pray, I was wrapped in the power of the Holy Spirit and was transported to California, standing in the grandmother's hospital room. I noticed that she was connected to many life-saving devices and appeared to be in a coma. I could see that demonic spirits had infiltrated her; this was a battle over her soul. Suddenly, I was back sitting on the sofa, praying with this young lady. The Lord then instructed me to tell her that He would arouse her grandmother's conscience so that someone could lead her to Him, in order for her to be saved.

The young lady erupted into tears and immediately called relatives in California, allowing me to speak with an aunt. I informed her that someone needed to remain at the hospital because this would be a short window of opportunity, and I was unaware of when this would occur. However, when her grandmother awakened from the coma, they must lead her in the salvation prayer immediately. This was a supernatural move of God. Sure enough, later that night, the grandmother gained consciousness, and they led her to Christ. Several days later, the grandmother passed away.

Hallelujah! The Lord was demonstrating what He had told me after the vision of hell. He desires that none be lost; He will save a soul up until the last breath. Though I was grieved that the grandmother had passed away, we had the assurance that she was with the Lord; He had snatched her out of the grip of the cohorts of hell. He is the lover of our souls.

Several days later, this young lady came to visit me and thank me before she traveled to the funeral services. I simply said, "Thank God; He is faithful." We prayed, and I hugged her. She fell out under the power of the Holy Spirit. I covered her with a blanket and let the Lord have His way. When she was able to get up, she was ecstatic, screaming, "I heard the Lord talking to me for the first time in my life! My grandmother is with Him!" We both erupted in praise and worship, tears, and unspeakable joy. I've been told that this young lady now seeks to know the Lord more personally and walks with Him more faithfully. Thank you, Lord! I love You so much, and I give You all the honor and adoration for the things You have done. Your goodness and mercy towards us never fail. How great You are!

One morning, as I sat at the table prepared for class, I asked the Lord why certain things had befallen me and my family. This began a week-long journey of revelation into the lives of my parents as well as myself. The Holy Spirit taught me how the evil one had caused much brokenness through traumas, trespasses, and temptation in humanity. As revealed in Ephesians 6:12, much devastation has occurred due to a lack of knowledge or understanding of this passage of scripture. Not understanding that we are not wrestling against flesh and blood physical opponents but against spiritual forces of wickedness has led to much destruction on many levels.

The Holy Spirit taught me about generational curses and the familiar spirits assigned to those curses, the structure of the kingdom of darkness, spiritual law, and the violation of that law. He also taught me about unforgiveness and how it takes root in a heart, and that when not uprooted, it turns into bitterness, which defiles many (Matthew 18:21-35). I learned about the spiritual and natural consequences of unforgiveness.

During this week of teaching, I received many visions about my family members and the body of Christ. I saw thousands of people sitting in Church very wounded, with fetters or nooses around their necks. They were saved and loved the Lord, but they were hindered from growing deeper or being called higher due to their woundedness and bondage. The broken hearts were enormous, and the Lord was saddened by this state of affairs. He said, "No more Church as usual; deliverance has been eradicated from My house, leaving many broken. I desire to unbreak their hearts."

Much of the teaching that week centered around Christ's earthly ministry, revealing the Father's heart and exposing the religious spirit. He, as well as His disciples, healed and delivered many throughout the New Testament. He revealed that there is a form of godliness void of power, just as He instructed the disciples to wait on the promise of the Father before beginning public ministry. This power is very necessary. That promise is the Baptism of the Holy Spirit. When I asked Him what I could do to assist in this dilemma, He replied, "Bring Heaven to earth! Teach the Kingdom of God; speak with authority and power. See what I AM doing and do it; hear what I AM saying and share it with those you minister to."

Again, I knew that without Him, I could do none of this. He continued, "Though many events in your life have been painful, you have been prepared." In that moment, it felt as if I went back through my life to when I was an infant, highlighting different events and the spiritual forces behind them. He revealed that I have always had the ability to discern the spiritual atmosphere, which is true. This gift has saved my life on many occasions. Though I could sense evil, I had never, until now, been able to see it.

One such event occurred many years ago when I worked in a psychiatric hospital. I was hosting a group counseling session with some adolescents when one of the children asked a question about God and their circumstances. As I attempted to explain the Scripture that her family had given her to read, a young man in the group jumped to his feet and dropped his pants. Of course, this startled everyone, and chaos erupted. I calmly instructed this young man to pull up his pants and go to his room. He looked at me with a piercing evil in his eyes and began to stand as if he was saluting something or someone, with his hand up to his head like a soldier. He began to speak a pledge to the Nazi flag, then unleashed a torrent of wild curse words at me.

I knew it was an evil spirit. As the other children ran out of the group room screaming and crying to the nurse's station, we called a code red. This means that other staff members working on that floor and others rush to the scene to assist and stabilize the patient. When a nurse came to the door to assist me, she informed me that she had called a code red. This lady, being a pastor's wife, and I simply said out loud, "Jesus, we need You." The young man then defecated into his hand, took off running, and began throwing feces at us as we followed behind him.

When we got to the end of the hallway and he had no

escape, he jumped up and began swinging from the exit sign, trying with great force to kick out the window, which was 6 or7 stories high, or the exit door, which had to be unlocked by a keypad code to protect patients and staff. By this time, several large men had come to our aid. We attempted to talk the young man down; however, he continued spewing profanities in what sounded like a different voice. Eventually, the men, after putting on protective gear, grabbed him and restrained him to the floor. You can imagine this was quite an unclean scene.

The unit was now locked down, requiring everyone to remain confined to their rooms for their protection. This young man was placed in an isolated padded room for the safety of himself and others until we could get orders from his doctor regarding how to treat him. Housekeeping then had to come and thoroughly clean the unit, as the children were taken to dinner.

After dinner, I went room to room with the nurse to complete mental health checks on everyone and dispense their medications. When we attempted to remove this young man to shower and medicate him per the doctor's orders, he was placed on what is called a one-on-one suicide watch, where a male staff member remained within arm's distance of him at all times. When he was taken to the restroom to shower, he dropped to his knees and attempted to drink from the toilet bowl, and he again had to be physically removed from the restroom.

He was then placed in a higher level of care in 4-point

restraints, meaning his arms and legs were secured by safety belts to each corner of the bed. When we attempted to medicate him, he spat on us, screaming profanity. When I returned to work the next day, I prayed from my car until I reached the floor. After checking in and getting briefed, my first priority was to check on the children. Some of them had called their families, begging them to take them out of there.

There was a flurry of activity: parents were calling to ensure their children were safe, and many different responses to these events emerged among the children. The psychiatric staff called an emergency meeting to discuss the event as well as the young man's current condition and determine the best course of action moving forward. As I explained how this all began and unfolded, it was determined that the level of care provided at this facility was not sufficient for this young man. Therefore, the process began to transfer him to a place I had been before: Austin Psychiatric Hospital.

Of course, this saddened my heart, for he was only a child, and I knew the evil that resided at that hospital. So, I decided to go and attempt to speak with and encourage him to take his medication so he could remain in this hospital. As I walked into the room, I could feel an evil presence there. The staff member got up, walked over to me, and began telling me about the day's events; I worked the 3 to 11 PM shift. He was lying quietly with his head facing the opposite direction. I assumed he was asleep when I began to speak. However, he turned his head toward me and became enraged, wrestling to get out of the restraints, hissing and screaming vile obscenities at me that had sexual content. Of course, I won't repeat this, but it was scary and shook me. I was literally trembling and saddened by his reaction to me. I came there with the purest intent to help this young man and save him from being transferred to a facility where everyone was in his condition.

My coworker could see the expression on my face, so he backed me out of the room and spoke with me from the doorway, where I was no longer visible to the young man, though he could keep his eyes on the patient while speaking to me. I continued working with the other children, but I could never forget this young man. The question in my heart was why he reacted to me in such a way. I love children, and usually, they love me. I knew I had not been unkind to this young man in any way, so this bothered me for a long time.

When I arrived at work the next day, they had placed him in a straitjacket and transported him out. I prayed for him; I never forgot him. Here now, 20 years later, the Holy Spirit is revealing the question in my heart concerning this young man, clarifying Ephesians 6:12: this young man needed deliverance, not medication, and it wasn't him we were wrestling with. His problem was spiritual in nature; therefore, it needed a spiritual solution. You can't remedy a spiritual problem with a physical solution, except it be temporary. It's like a Band-Aid being placed on a gunshot wound—it can't assist in the healing until the bullet is removed. It must be removed internally in order for the wound to heal externally.

This led to much revelation and teaching about disease and spirits causing infirmities in the body, and why many times they go unhealed, or why mental illness continues to recur without true healing at times. I must say that not every ill person needs deliverance; however, some do, such as this young man.

Another day's lessons revealed how very differently I thought as opposed to God. I realized that both myself and most human beings see and judge life and others based on our own understanding (Proverbs 3:5-6). Though I loved the Lord as much as I was capable at that time, I, being the sum total of my life experiences, saw life and people through my pain, which failed in comparison to God's. The Holy Spirit began to teach me about judging and the spiritual principle of sowing and reaping. As the Holy Spirit revealed the heart of the Father, I recognized the vast difference between my understanding and His, as far apart as the heavens are from the earth. This led to a week of repentance, during which I renounced many vows and judgments I had made throughout my life over painful experiences, as well as the effects of those hurts on my heart, mind, and soul, bringing more deliverance for me. The Holy Spirit revealed again that man looks on the outward appearance and behavior, but the Lord looks upon the heart of a person. He also knows that person's life history and the sum total of their life experiences; therefore, He has compassion and mercy towards them, understanding what caused them to think and behave as they do—just as I had.

Living in a fallen world full of sin and Satan is why He continued to tell me to stop striving for His approval, stating that we are loved exceedingly above what we can think or imagine. This love, which you've already been given, is untainted; it IS, and there is no need to strive for it. As you love your children, the Holy Spirit revealed that they didn't strive to be loved; they were born loved, even when their behavior displeases you. Because you want the best for them, your love for them never fades. The issue is not whether God loves us—He IS love. The issue is that His children are unaware of His great love for them, just as you may be.

The Holy Spirit showed me how the brokenness of our natural fathers' love was projected onto Him. Humans were created to give and receive love unconditionally. The big dilemma is that we can only give what we have. In order to give love, one must first receive love. If you need 1000 dollars and I only have 500 hundred dollars, even if I lovingly give you all that I have, it still isn't enough to meet your need. You would still be $500 hundred dollars deficient in your requirement. People, no matter who they are, including parents, can only give us what they have received. This has led to striving for the filling of our love tanks and all sorts of woundedness and destruction.

He was calling me out of the world system into the Kingdom of God, which required a death to who I was at that time. Of course, truth changes facts, or the facts to which I may be limited at any given time; Jesus Christ is the truth. I am learning to live His way so that I may truly experience life.

I've learned to inquire of the Lord as opposed to leaning on my own understanding. However, I must say that at times this is a very painful process, called renewing the mind (Romans 12:2; Proverbs 23:7). Dying to my thinking patterns and the idolatry of self, along with the deception and pride associated with my belief that I know best apart from God's viewpoint, is challenging. While enrolled in the school of the Holy Spirit, I thought I understood these revelations—what an understatement! What I didn't realize at that time was the process necessary to bring revelation from my mind to my heart and to learn to live them out in daily life, in a fallen world filled with broken people, including myself, who had not yet received these truths.

I can say with all honesty today that I am nothing without God. The things God revealed to me over a decade ago, I'm still having to live out to clearly understand. When God speaks, it requires time to grow into absolute truth, or it has for me, as I learn to keep my mind focused on Christ's ministry or to be sanctified into the mind of Christ. I thank Him daily that I don't have to learn alone. Jesus is our friend who sticks closer than a brother. He is the author and finisher of our faith, the good shepherd, and the good work He has begun in us He will complete!!

Made in the USA
Middletown, DE
12 January 2025

68507742R00046